P9-DMU-149

SAND AND FOAM

The Books of
KAHLIL GIBRAN

"His power came from some great reservoir of spiritual life
else it could not have been so universal and so potent, but
the majesty and beauty of the language with which he clothed
it were all his own." — CLAUDE BRAGDON

The Madman · 1918

Twenty Drawings · 1919

The Forerunner · 1920

The Prophet · 1923

Sand and Foam · 1926

Jesus the Son of Man · 1928

The Earth Gods · 1931

The Wanderer · 1932

The Garden of the Prophet · 1933

Prose Poems · 1934

Nymphs of the Valley · 1948

Spirits Rebellious · 1948

A Tear and a Smile · 1950

∵

Beloved Prophet
The Love Letters of
Kahlil Gibran and Mary Haskell
Edited by Virginia Hilu

This Man from Lebanon—
A Study of Kahlil Gibran
by Barbara Young

PUBLISHED BY ALFRED A. KNOPF

SAND
AND FOAM

A Book of Aphorisms

BY

KAHLIL GIBRAN

1981

NEW YORK : ALFRED·A·KNOPF

COPYRIGHT, 1926, BY KAHLIL GIBRAN

*Renewal copyright 1954 by Administrators C. T. A.
of Kahlil Gibran Estate and Mary G. Gibran*

*All rights reserved under International and Pan-American
Copyright Conventions. Published in the United States by
Alfred A. Knopf, Inc., New York, and distributed by Random
House, Inc., New York.*

PUBLISHED OCTOBER 1926
REPRINTED THIRTY-FIVE TIMES
THIRTY-SEVENTH PRINTING, MAY 1981

THIS IS A BORZOI BOOK,
PUBLISHED BY ALFRED A. KNOPF, INC.

MANUFACTURED IN THE UNITED STATES OF AMERICA

THE SEVEN ILLUSTRATIONS
IN THIS VOLUME ARE RE-
PRODUCED FROM ORIGINAL
DRAWINGS BY THE AUTHOR

SAND AND FOAM

I am forever walking upon these shores,
Betwixt the sand and the foam.
The high tide will erase my foot-prints,
And the wind will blow away the foam.
But the sea and the shore will remain
Forever.

Once I filled my hand with mist.

Then I opened it and lo, the mist was a worm.

And I closed and opened my hand again, and behold there was a bird.

And again I closed and opened my hand, and in its hollow stood a man with a sad face, turned upward.

And again I closed my hand, and when I opened it there was naught but mist.

But I heard a song of exceeding sweetness.

It was but yesterday I thought myself a fragment quivering without rhythm in the sphere of life.

Now I know that I am the sphere, and all life in rhythmic fragments moves within me.

They say to me in their awakening, "You and the world you live in are but a grain of sand upon the infinite shore of an infinite sea."

And in my dream I say to them, "I am the infinite sea, and all worlds are but grains of sand upon my shore."

Only once have I been made mute.   It was when a man asked me, "Who are you?"

The first thought of God was an angel.
The first word of God was a man.

We were fluttering, wandering, long-ing creatures a thousand thousand years before the sea and the wind in the forest gave us words.

Now how can we express the ancient of days in us with only the sounds of our yesterdays?

The Sphinx spoke only once, and the Sphinx said, "A grain of sand is a desert, and a desert is a grain of sand; and now let us all be silent again."

I heard the Sphinx, but I did not understand.

3

Once I saw the face of a woman, and I beheld all her children not yet born.

And a woman looked upon my face and she knew all my forefathers, dead before she was born.

Now would I fulfill myself.   But how shall I unless I become a planet with intelligent lives dwelling upon it?

Is not this every man's goal?

A pearl is a temple built by pain around a grain of sand.

What longing built our bodies and around what grains?

When God threw me, a pebble, into this wondrous lake I disturbed its surface with countless circles.

But when I reached the depths I became very still.

Give me silence and I will outdare the night.

I had a second birth when my soul and my body loved one another and were married.

Once I knew a man whose ears were exceedingly keen, but he was dumb. He had lost his tongue in a battle.

I know now what battles that man fought before the great silence came. I am glad he is dead.

The world is not large enough for two of us.

Long did I lie in the dust of Egypt, silent and unaware of the seasons.

Then the sun gave me birth, and I rose and walked upon the banks of the Nile,

Singing with the days and dreaming with the nights.

And now the sun treads upon me with a thousand feet that I may lie again in the dust of Egypt.

But behold a marvel and a riddle!

The very sun that gathered me cannot scatter me.

Still erect am I, and sure of foot do I walk upon the banks of the Nile.

Remembrance is a form of meeting.

Forgetfulness is a form of freedom.

We measure time according to the movement of countless suns; and they measure time by little machines in their little pockets.

Now tell me, how could we ever meet at the same place and the same time?

Space is not space between the earth and the sun to one who looks down from the windows of the Milky Way.

Humanity is a river of light running from ex-eternity to eternity.

Do not the spirits who dwell in the ether envy man his pain?

On my way to the Holy City I met another pilgrim and I asked him, "Is this indeed the way to the Holy City?"

And he said, "Follow me, and you will reach the Holy City in a day and a night."

And I followed him. And we walked many days and many nights, yet we did not reach the Holy City.

And what was to my surprise he became angry with me because he had misled me.

Make me, oh God, the prey of the lion, ere You make the rabbit my prey.

One may not reach the dawn save by the path of the night.

My house says to me, "Do not leave me, for here dwells your past."

And the road says to me, "Come and follow me, for I am your future."

And I say to both my house and the road, "I have no past, nor have I a future. If I stay here, there is a going in my staying; and if I go there is a staying in my going. Only love and death change all things."

How can I lose faith in the justice of life, when the dreams of those who sleep upon feathers are not more beautiful than the dreams of those who sleep upon the earth?

Strange, the desire for certain pleasures is a part of my pain.

9

Seven times have I despised my soul:

The first time when I saw her being meek that she might attain height.

The second time when I saw her limping before the crippled.

The third time when she was given to choose between the hard and the easy, and she chose the easy.

The fourth time when she committed a wrong, and comforted herself that others also commit wrong.

The fifth time when she forbore for weakness, and attributed her patience to strength.

The sixth time when she despised the ugliness of a face, and knew not that it was one of her own masks.

And the seventh time when she sang a song of praise, and deemed it a virtue.

I am ignorant of absolute truth.   But I am humble before my ignorance and therein lies my honor and my reward.

There is a space between man's imagination and man's attainment that may only be traversed by his longing.

Paradise is there, behind that door, in the next room; but I have lost the key. Perhaps I have only mislaid it.

You are blind and I am deaf and dumb, so let us touch hands and understand.

The significance of man is not in what he attains, but rather in what he longs to attain.

Some of us are like ink and some like paper.

And if it were not for the blackness of some of us, some of us would be dumb;

And if it were not for the whiteness of some of us, some of us would be blind.

Give me an ear and I will give you a voice.

Our mind is a sponge; our heart is a stream.

Is it not strange that most of us choose sucking rather than running?

When you long for blessings that you may not name, and when you grieve knowing not the cause, then indeed you are growing with all things that grow, and rising toward your greater self.

When one is drunk with a vision, he deems his faint expression of it the very wine.

You drink wine that you may be intoxicated; and I drink that it may sober me from that other wine.

When my cup is empty I resign myself to its emptiness; but when it is half full I resent its half-fulness.

The reality of the other person is not in what he reveals to you, but in what he cannot reveal to you.

Therefore, if you would understand him, listen not to what he says but rather to what he does not say.

Half of what I say is meaningless; but I say it so that the other half may reach you.

A sense of humor is a sense of proportion.

My loneliness was born when men praised my talkative faults and blamed my silent virtues.

When Life does not find a singer to sing her heart she produces a philosopher to speak her mind.

A truth is to be known always, to be uttered sometimes.

The real in us is silent; the acquired is talkative.

The voice of life in me cannot reach the ear of life in you; but let us talk that we may not feel lonely.

When two women talk they say nothing; when one woman speaks she reveals all of life.

Frogs may bellow louder than bulls, but they cannot drag the plough in the field nor turn the wheel of the winepress, and of their skins you cannot make shoes.

Only the dumb envy the talkative.

If winter should say, "Spring is in my heart," who would believe winter?

Every seed is a longing.

Should you really open your eyes and see, you would behold your image in all images.

And should you open your ears and listen, you would hear your own voice in all voices.

It takes two of us to discover truth: one to utter it and one to understand it.

Though the wave of words is forever upon us, yet our depth is forever silent.

Many a doctrine is like a window pane. We see truth through it but it divides us from truth.

17

Now let us play hide and seek. Should you hide in my heart it would not be difficult to find you. But should you hide behind your own shell, then it would be useless for anyone to seek you.

A woman may veil her face with a smile.

How noble is the sad heart who would sing a joyous song with joyous hearts.

He who would understand a woman, or dissect genius, or solve the mystery of silence is the very man who would wake from a beautiful dream to sit at a breakfast table.

I would walk with all those who walk. I would not stand still to watch the procession passing by.

You owe more than gold to him who serves you. Give him of your heart or serve him.

Nay, we have not lived in vain. Have they not built towers of our bones?

Let us not be particular and sectional. The poet's mind and the scorpion's tail rise in glory from the same earth.

Every dragon gives birth to a St. George who slays it.

19

Trees are poems that the earth writes upon the sky. We fell them down and turn them into paper that we may record our emptiness.

Should you care to write (and only the saints know why you should) you must needs have knowledge and art and magic —the knowledge of the music of words, the art of being artless, and the magic of loving your readers.

They dip their pens in our hearts and think they are inspired.

Should a tree write its autobiography it would not be unlike the history of a race.

If I were to choose between the power of writing a poem and the ecstasy of a poem unwritten, I would choose the ecstasy. It is better poetry.

But you and all my neighbors agree that I always choose badly.

Poetry is not an opinion expressed. It is a song that rises from a bleeding wound or a smiling mouth.

Words are timeless. You should utter them or write them with a knowledge of their timelessness.

A poet is a dethroned king sitting among the ashes of his palace trying to fashion an image out of the ashes.

21

Poetry is a deal of joy and pain and wonder, with a dash of the dictionary.

In vain shall a poet seek the mother of the songs of his heart.

Once I said to a poet, "We shall not know your worth until you die."

And he answered saying, "Yes, death is always the revealer. And if indeed you would know my worth it is that I have more in my heart than upon my tongue, and more in my desire than in my hand."

If you sing of beauty though alone in the heart of the desert you will have an audience.

Poetry is wisdom that enchants the heart.

Wisdom is poetry that sings in the mind.

If we could enchant man's heart and at the same time sing in his mind,

Then in truth he would live in the shadow of God.

Inspiration will always sing; inspiration will never explain.

We often sing lullabyes to our children that we ourselves may sleep.

All our words are but crumbs that fall down from the feast of the mind.

23

Thinking is always the stumbling stone to poetry.

A great singer is he who sings our silences.

How can you sing if your mouth be filled with food?

How shall your hand be raised in blessing if it is filled with gold?

They say the nightingale pierces his bosom with a thorn when he sings his love song.

So do we all. How else should we sing?

Genius is but a robin's song at the beginning of a slow spring.

Even the most winged spirit cannot escape physical necessity.

A madman is not less a musician than you or myself; only the instrument on which he plays is a little out of tune.

The song that lies silent in the heart of a mother sings upon the lips of her child.

No longing remains unfulfilled.

I have never agreed with my other self wholly. The truth of the matter seems to lie between us.

Your other self is always sorry for you. But your other self grows on sorrow; so all is well.

There is no struggle of soul and body save in the minds of those whose souls are asleep and whose bodies are out of tune.

When you reach the heart of life you shall find beauty in all things, even in the eyes that are blind to beauty.

26

We live only to discover beauty. All else is a form of waiting.

Sow a seed and the earth will yield you a flower. Dream your dream to the sky and it will bring you your beloved.

The devil died the very day you were born.

Now you do not have to go through hell to meet an angel.

Many a woman borrows a man's heart; very few could possess it.

If you would possess you must not claim.

27

When a man's hand touches the hand of a woman they both touch the heart of eternity.

Love is the veil between lover and lover.

Every man loves two women; the one is the creation of his imagination, and the other is not yet born.

Men who do not forgive women their little faults will never enjoy their great virtues.

Love that does not renew itself every day becomes a habit and in turn a slavery.

Lovers embrace that which is between them rather than each other.

Love and doubt have never been on speaking terms.

Love is a word of light, written by a hand of light, upon a page of light.

Friendship is always a sweet responsibility, never an opportunity.

If you do not understand your friend under all conditions you will never understand him.

Your most radiant garment is of the other person's weaving;

Your most savory meal is that which you eat at the other person's table;

Your most comfortable bed is in the other person's house.

Now tell me, how can you separate yourself from the other person?

Your mind and my heart will never agree until your mind ceases to live in numbers and my heart in the mist.

We shall never understand one another until we reduce the language to seven words.

How shall my heart be unsealed unless it be broken?

Only great sorrow or great joy can reveal your truth.

If you would be revealed you must either dance naked in the sun, or carry your cross.

Should nature heed what we say of contentment no river would seek the sea, and no winter would turn to Spring. Should she heed all we say of thrift, how many of us would be breathing this air?

You see but your shadow when you turn your back to the sun.

31

You are free before the sun of the day, and free before the stars of the night;

And you are free when there is no sun and no moon and no star.

You are even free when you close your eyes upon all there is.

But you are a slave to him whom you love because you love him,

And a slave to him who loves you because he loves you.

We are all beggars at the gate of the temple, and each one of us receives his share of the bounty of the King when he enters the temple, and when he goes out.

But we are all jealous of one another, which is another way of belittling the King.

You cannot consume beyond your appetite. The other half of the loaf belongs to the other person, and there should remain a little bread for the chance guest.

If it were not for guests all houses would be graves.

Said a gracious wolf to a simple sheep, "Will you not honor our house with a visit?"

And the sheep answered: "We would have been honored to visit your house if it were not in your stomach."

I stopped my guest on the threshold and said, "Nay, wipe not your feet as you enter, but as you go out."

Generosity is not in giving me that which I need more than you do, but it is in giving me that which you need more than I do.

You are indeed charitable when you give, and while giving, turn your face away so that you may not see the shyness of the receiver.

The difference between the richest man and the poorest is but a day of hunger and an hour of thirst.

We often borrow from our tomorrows to pay our debts to our yesterdays.

I too am visited by angels and devils, but I get rid of them.

When it is an angel I pray an old prayer, and he is bored;

When it is a devil I commit an old sin, and he passes me by.

After all this is not a bad prison; but I do not like this wall between my cell and the next prisoner's cell;

Yet I assure you that I do not wish to reproach the warder nor the Builder of the prison.

Those who give you a serpent when you ask for a fish, may have nothing but serpents to give. It is then generosity on their part.

Trickery succeeds sometimes, but it always commits suicide.

You are truly a forgiver when you forgive murderers who never spill blood, thieves who never steal, and liars who utter no falsehood.

He who can put his finger upon that which divides good from evil is he who can touch the very hem of the garment of God.

If your heart is a volcano how shall you expect flowers to bloom in your hands?

36

A strange form of self-indulgence! There are times when I would be wronged and cheated, that I may laugh at the expense of those who think I do not know I am being wronged and cheated.

What shall I say of him who is the pursuer playing the part of the pursued?

Let him who wipes his soiled hands with your garment take your garment. He may need it again; surely you would not.

It is a pity that money-changers cannot be good gardners.

Please do not whitewash your inherent faults with your acquired virtues. I would have the faults; they are like mine own.

How often have I attributed to myself crimes I have never committed, so that the other person may feel comfortable in my presence.

Even the masks of life are masks of deeper mystery.

You may judge others only according to your knowledge of yourself.

Tell me now, who among us is guilty and who is unguilty?

The truly just is he who feels half guilty of your misdeeds.

Only an idiot and a genius break man-made laws; and they are the nearest to the heart of God.

It is only when you are pursued that you become swift.

I have no enemies, O God, but if I am to have an enemy
 Let his strength be equal to mine,
 That truth alone may be the victor.

You will be quite friendly with your enemy when you both die.

Perhaps a man may commit suicide in self-defense.

Long ago there lived a Man who was crucified for being too loving and too lovable.

And strange to relate I met him thrice yesterday.

The first time He was asking a policeman not to take a prostitute to prison; the second time He was drinking wine with an outcast; and the third time He was having a fist-fight with a promoter inside a church.

If all they say of good and evil were true, then my life is but one long crime.

Pity is but half justice.

The only one who has been unjust to me is the one to whose brother I have been unjust.

When you see a man led to prison say in your heart, "Mayhap he is escaping from a narrower prison."

And when you see a man drunken say in your heart, "Mayhap he sought escape from something still more unbeautiful."

Oftentimes I have hated in self-defense; but if I were stronger I would not have used such a weapon.

How stupid is he who would patch the hatred in his eyes with the smile of his lips.

Only those beneath me can envy or hate me.

I have never been envied nor hated; I am above no one.

Only those above me can praise or belittle me.

I have never been praised nor belittled; I am below no one.

Your saying to me, "I do not understand you," is praise beyond my worth, and an insult you do not deserve.

How mean am I when life gives me gold and I give you silver, and yet I deem myself generous.

When you reach the heart of life you will find yourself not higher than the felon, and not lower than the prophet.

Strange that you should pity the slow-footed and not the slow-minded,

And the blind-eyed rather than the blind-hearted.

It is wiser for the lame not to break his crutches upon the head of his enemy.

How blind is he who gives you out of his pocket that he may take out of your heart.

Life is a procession. The slow of foot finds it too swift and he steps out;

And the swift of foot finds it too slow and he too steps out.

If there is such a thing as sin some of us commit it backward following our fore-fathers footsteps;

And some of us commit it forward by overruling our children.

The truly good is he who is one with all those who are deemed bad.

We are all prisoners but some of us are in cells with windows and some without.

Strange that we all defend our wrongs with more vigor than we do our rights.

Should we all confess our sins to one another we would all laugh at one another
for our lack of originality.

Should we all reveal our virtues we
would also laugh for the same cause.

An individual is above man-made laws
until he commits a crime against man-
made conventions;

After that he is neither above anyone
nor lower than anyone.

Government is an agreement between
you and myself. You and myself are
often wrong.

Crime is either another name of need or
an aspect of a disease.

Is there a greater fault than being conscious of the other person's faults?

If the other person laughs at you, you can pity him; but if you laugh at him you may never forgive yourself.

If the other person injures you, you may forget the injury; but if you injure him you will always remember.

In truth the other person is your most sensitive self given another body.

How heedless you are when you would have men fly with your wings and you cannot even give them a feather.

46

Once a man sat at my board and ate my bread and drank my wine and went away laughing at me.

Then he came again for bread and wine, and I spurned him;

And the angels laughed at me.

Hate is a dead thing. Who of you would be a tomb?

It is the honor of the murdered that he is not the murderer.

The tribune of humanity is in its silent heart never its talkative mind.

They deem me mad because I will not
sell my days for gold;

And I deem them mad because they
think my days have a price.

They spread before us their riches of
gold and silver, of ivory and ebony, and
we spread before them our hearts and our
spirits;

And yet they deem themselves the hosts
and us the guests.

I would be the least among men with
dreams and the desire to fulfill them,
rather than the greatest with no dreams
and no desires.

The most pitiful among men is he who turns his dreams into silver and gold.

We are all climbing toward the summit of our hearts' desire. Should the other climber steal your sack and your purse and wax fat on the one and heavy on the other, you should pity him;

The climbing will be harder for his flesh, and the burden will make his way longer.

And should you in your leanness see his flesh puffing upward, help him a step; it will add to your swiftness.

You cannot judge any man beyond your knowledge of him, and how small is your knowledge.

I would not listen to a conqueror preaching to the conquered.

The truly free man is he who bears the load of the bond slave patiently.

A thousand years ago my neighbor said to me, "I hate life, for it is naught but a thing of pain."

And yesterday I passed by a cemetery and saw life dancing upon his grave.

Strife in nature is but disorder longing for order.

Solitude is a silent storm that breaks down all our dead branches;

Yet it sends our living roots deeper into the living heart of the living earth.

Once I spoke of the sea to a brook, and the brook thought me but an imaginative exaggerator;

And once I spoke of a brook to the sea, and the sea thought me but a depreciative defamer.

How narrow is the vision that exalts the busyness of the ant above the singing of the grasshopper.

The highest virtue here may be the least in another world.

The deep and the high go to the depth or to the height in a straight line; only the spacious can move in circles.

If it were not for our conception of weights and measures we would stand in awe of the firefly as we do before the sun.

A scientist without imagination is a butcher with dull knives and out-worn scales.

But what would you, since we are not all vegetarians?

When you sing the hungry hears you with his stomach.

Death is not nearer to the aged than to the new-born; neither is life.

If indeed you must be candid, be candid beautifully; otherwise keep silent, for there is a man in our neighborhood who is dying.

Mayhap a funeral among men is a wedding feast among the angels.

A forgotten reality may die and leave in its will seven thousand actualities and facts to be spent in its funeral and the building of a tomb.

In truth we talk only to ourselves, but sometimes we talk loud enough that others may hear us.

The obvious is that which is never seen until someone expresses it simply.

If the Milky Way were not within me how should I have seen it or known it?

Unless I am a physician among physicians they would not believe that I am an astronomer.

Perhaps the sea's definition of a shell is the pearl.

Perhaps time's definition of coal is the diamond.

Fame is the shadow of passion standing in the light.

A root is a flower that disdains fame.

There is neither religion nor science beyond beauty.

Every great man I have known had something small in his make-up; and it was that small something which prevented inactivity or madness or suicide.

The truly great man is he who would master no one, and who would be mastered by none.

I would not believe that man is a mediocre simply because he kills the criminals and the prophets.

Tolerance is love sick with the sickness of haughtiness.

Worms will turn; but is it not strange that even elephants will yield?

A disagreement may be the shortest cut between two minds.

I am the flame and I am the dry brush, and one part of me consumes the other part.

We are all seeking the summit of the holy mountain; but shall not our road be shorter if we consider the past a chart and not a guide?

Wisdom ceases to be wisdom when it becomes too proud to weep, too grave to laugh, and too self-ful to seek other than itself.

Had I filled myself with all that you know what room should I have for all that you do not know?

I have learned silence from the talkative, toleration from the intolerant, and kindness from the unkind; yet strange, I am ungrateful to these teachers.

A bigot is a stone-deaf orator.

The silence of the envious is too noisy.

When you reach the end of what you should know, you will be at the beginning of what you should sense.

An exaggeration is a truth that has lost its temper.

If you can see only what light reveals and hear only what sound announces,
Then in truth you do not see nor do you hear.

A fact is a truth unsexed.

You cannot laugh and be unkind at the same time.

The nearest to my heart are a king without a kingdom and a poor man who does not know how to beg.

A shy failure is nobler than an immodest success.

Dig anywhere in the earth and you will find a treasure, only you must dig with the faith of a peasant.

Said a hunted fox followed by twenty
horsemen and a pack of twenty hounds,
"Of course they will kill me. But how
poor and how stupid they must be.
Surely it would not be worth while for
twenty foxes riding on twenty asses and
accompanied by twenty wolves to chase
and kill one man."

It is the mind in us that yields to the
laws made by us, but never the spirit
in us.

A traveler am I and a navigator, and
every day I discover a new region within
my soul.

A woman protested saying, "Of course it was a righteous war. My son fell in it."

I said to Life, "I would hear Death speak."

And Life raised her voice a little higher and said, "You hear him now."

When you have solved all the mysteries of life you long for death, for it is but another mystery of life.

Birth and death are the two noblest expressions of bravery.

My friend, you and I shall remain
strangers unto life,

And unto one another, and each unto
himself,

Until the day when you shall speak and
and I shall listen

Deeming your voice my own voice;

And when I shall stand before you

Thinking myself standing before a
mirror.

They say to me, "Should you know
yourself you would know all men."

And I say, "Only when I seek all men
shall I know myself."

Man is two men; one is awake in dark-
ness, the other is asleep in light.

A hermit is one who renounces the world of fragments that he may enjoy the world wholly and without interruption.

There lies a green field between the scholar and the poet; should the scholar cross it he becomes a wise man; should the poet cross it, he becomes a prophet.

Yestereve I saw philosophers in the market-place carrying their heads in baskets, and crying aloud, "Wisdom! Wisdom for sale!"

Poor philosophers! They must needs sell their heads to feed their hearts.

Said a philosopher to a street sweeper, "I pity you. Yours is a hard and dirty task."

And the street sweeper said, "Thank you, sir. But tell me what is your task?"

And the philosopher answered saying, "I study man's mind, his deeds and his desires."

Then the street sweeper went on with his sweeping and said with a smile, "I pity you too."

He who listens to truth is not less than he who utters truth.

No man can draw the line between necessities and luxuries. Only the angels can do that, and the angels are wise and wistful.

Perhaps the angels are our better thoughts in space.

He is the true prince who finds his throne in the heart of the dervish.

Generosity is giving more than you can, and pride is taking less than you need.

In truth you owe naught to any man. You owe all to all men.

All those who have lived in the past live with us now. Surely none of us would be an ungracious host.

He who longs the most lives the longest.

66

They say to me, "A bird in the hand is worth ten in the bush."

But I say, "A bird and a feather in the bush is worth more than ten birds in the hand."

Your seeking after *that feather* is life with winged feet; nay, it is life itself.

There are only two elements here, beauty and truth; beauty in the hearts of lovers, and truth in the arms of the tillers of the soil.

Great beauty captures me, but a beauty still greater frees me even from itself.

Beauty shines brighter in the heart of him who longs for it than in the eyes of him who sees it.

I admire the man who reveals his mind to me; I honor him who unveils his dreams. But why am I shy, and even a little ashamed before him who serves me?

The gifted were once proud in serving princes.

Now they claim honor in serving paupers.

The angels know that too many practical men eat their bread with the sweat of the dreamer's brow.

Wit is often a mask. If you could tear it you would find either a genius irritated or cleverness juggling.

The understanding attributes to me understanding and the dull, dullness. I think they are both right.

Only those with secrets in their hearts could divine the secrets in our hearts.

He who would share your pleasure but not your pain shall lose the key to one of the seven gates of Paradise.

Yes, there is a Nirvanah; it is in leading your sheep to a green pasture, and in putting your child to sleep, and in writing the last line of your poem.

We choose our joys and our sorrows long before we experience them.

Sadness is but a wall between two gardens.

When either your joy or your sorrow becomes great the world becomes small.

Desire is half of life; indifference is half of death.

The bitterest thing in our today's sorrow is the memory of our yesterday's joy.

They say to me, "You must needs choose between the pleasures of this world and the peace of the next world."

And I say to them, "I have chosen both the delights of this world and the peace of the next. For I know in my heart that the Supreme Poet wrote but one poem, and it scans perfectly, and it also rhymes perfectly."

Faith is an oasis in the heart which will never be reached by the caravan of thinking.

When you reach your height you shall desire but only for desire; and you shall hunger, for hunger; and you shall thirst for greater thirst.

If you reveal your secrets to the wind you should not blame the wind for revealing them to the trees.

The flowers of spring are winter's dreams related at the breakfast table of the angels.

Said a skunk to a tube-rose, "See how swiftly I run, while you cannot walk nor even creep."

Said the tube-rose to the skunk, "Oh, most noble swift runner, please run swiftly!"

Turtles can tell more about the roads than hares.

Strange that creatures without backbones have the hardest shells.

The most talkative is the least intelligent, and there is hardly a difference between an orator and an auctioneer.

Be grateful that you do not have to live down the renown of a father nor the wealth of an uncle.

But above all be grateful that no one will have to live down either your renown or your wealth.

Only when a juggler misses catching his ball does he appeal to me.

The envious praises me unknowingly.

Long were you a dream in your mother's sleep, and then she woke to give you birth.

The germ of the race is in your mother's longing.

My father and mother desired a child and they begot me.

And I wanted a mother and a father and I begot night and the sea.

Some of our children are our justifications and some are but our regrets.

When night comes and you too are dark, lie down and be dark with a will.

And when morning comes and you are still dark stand up and say to the day with a will, "I am still dark."

It is stupid to play a rôle with the night and the day.

They would both laugh at you.

The mountain veiled in mist is not a hill; an oak tree in the rain is not a weeping willow.

Behold here is a paradox: the deep and high are nearer to one another than the mid-level to either.

When I stood a clear mirror before you,
you gazed into me and saw your image.
Then you said, "I love you."
But in truth you loved yourself in me.

When you enjoy loving your neighbor
it ceases to be a virtue.

Love which is not always springing is
always dying.

You cannot have youth and the knowledge of it at the same time;
For youth is too busy living to know,
and knowledge is too busy seeking itself
to live.

You may sit at your window watching the passersby. And watching you may see a nun walking toward your right hand, and a prostitute toward your left hand.

And you may say in your innocence, "How noble is the one and how ignoble is the other."

But should you close your eyes and listen awhile you would hear a voice whispering in the ether, "One seeks me in prayer, and the other in pain. And in the spirit of each there is a bower for my spirit."

Once every hundred years Jesus of Nazareth meets Jesus of the Christian in a garden among the hills of Lebanon. And they talk long; and each time Jesus of Nazareth goes away saying to Jesus of the Christian, "My friend, I fear we shall never, never agree."

May God feed the over-abundant!

A great man has two hearts; one bleeds and the other forbears.

Should one tell a lie which does not hurt you nor anyone else, why not say in your heart that the house of his facts is too small for his fancies, and he had to leave it for larger space?

Behind every closed door is a mystery sealed with seven seals.

Waiting is the hoofs of time.

What if trouble should be a new window in the Eastern wall of your house?

You may forget the one with whom you have laughed, but never the one with whom you have wept.

There must be something strangely sacred in salt. It is in our tears and in the sea.

Our God in His gracious thirst will drink us all, the dewdrop and the tear.

79

You are but a fragment of your giant self, a mouth that seeks bread, and a blind hand that holds the cup for a thirsty mouth.

If you would rise but a cubit above race and country and self you would indeed become godlike.

If I were you I would not find fault with the sea at low tide.

It is a good ship and our Captain is able; it is only your stomach that is in disorder.

What we long for and cannot attain is dearer than what we have already attained.

Should you sit upon a cloud you would not see the boundary line between one country and another, nor the boundary stone between a farm and a farm.

It is a pity you cannot sit upon a cloud.

Seven centuries ago seven white doves rose from a deep valley flying to the snow-white summit of the mountain. One of the seven men who watched the flight said, "I see a black spot on the wing of the seventh dove."

Today the people in that valley tell of seven black doves that flew to the summit of the snowy mountain.

81

In the autumn I gathered all my sorrows and buried them in my garden.

And when April returned and spring came to wed the earth, there grew in my garden beautiful flowers unlike all other flowers.

And my neighbors came to behold them, and they all said to me, "When autumn comes again, at seeding time, will you not give us of the seeds of these flowers that we may have them in our gardens?"

It is indeed misery if I stretch an empty hand to men and receive nothing; but it is hopelessness if I stretch a full hand and find none to receive.

I long for eternity because there I shall meet my unwritten poems and my unpainted pictures.

Art is a step from nature toward the Infinite.

A work of art is a mist carved into an image.

Even the hands that make crowns of thorns are better than idle hands.

Our most sacred tears never seek our eyes.

Every man is the descendant of every king and every slave that ever lived.

If the great-grandfather of Jesus had known what was hidden within him, would he not have stood in awe of himself?

Was the love of Judas' mother for her son less than the love of Mary for Jesus?

There are three miracles of our Brother Jesus not yet recorded in the Book: the first that He was a man like you and me; the second that He had a sense of humor; and the third that He knew He was a conqueror though conquered.

Crucified One, you are crucified upon my heart; and the nails that pierce your hands pierce the walls of my heart.

And tomorrow when a stranger passes by this Golgotha he will not know that two bled here.

He will deem it the blood of one man.

You may have heard of the Blessed Mountain.

It is the highest mountain in our world.

Should you reach the summit you would have only one desire, and that to descend and be with those who dwell in the deepest valley.

That is why it is called the Blessed Mountain.

Every thought I have imprisoned in expression I must free by my deeds.

A NOTE ON THE TYPE IN
WHICH THIS BOOK IS SET

This book is set (on the Linotype) in Original Old Style of the history of which very little is known; in practically its present form, it has been used for many years for fine book and magazine work. The design of its lower case letters would indicate a derivation from English and Dutch Old Styles of the seventeenth and early eighteenth centuries, the period which reached its culmination in the work of William Caslon. The blackness of its capitals shows clearly, however, that their design was modified in imitation of the Modern faces which so completely displaced the Old Styles during the first half of the nineteenth century. Original Old Style possesses in a high degree those two qualities by which a book type must be judged: first, legibility, and second, the ability to impart a definite character to a page without intruding itself upon the reader's consciousness.